Contents Page

Published by Step Forward Publishing Limited
St Jude's Church, Dulwich Road, Herne Hill, London, SE24 0PB
Tel: 020 7738 5454 www.practicalpreschool.com
© Step Forward Publishing Limited 2008   Illustrations by Cathy Hughes
ISBN 13: 978 1904575 38 2

Stepping Stones to Creativity

Stepping Stones to Creativity is a series of books that aim to provide early years practitioners with a treasure trove of practical activities and resources to help develop the budding creativity of children in their care. Each book focuses on a different area of creativity, which is explored through forty of the most popular early years topics. In each topic you will find activities that are linked to the five Early Learning Goals of Creative Development so that you can ensure you are meeting the requirements of the Early Years Foundation Stage.

Many of these activities can be adapted for even younger children or extended to benefit Key Stage One children.

Creativity In The Classroom

Creativity is an elusive term. Although great enjoyment can be taken from working with imaginative children in the Early Years who are naturally eager to explore, in practice there are some key issues which face the practitioner:

What is 'creativity'?

In a nutshell, it is the ability to use knowledge and skills, plus a healthy dollop of imagination, to tackle and solve any problem. It is about taking risks and being involved in the learning process. Creative thinking does not just apply to obviously 'creative' tasks such as art or music, but can be used in investigations in science and across the foundation stage curriculum. To develop creativity children need time, space, and multiple opportunities to experiment with materials and ideas. They also need to be encouraged to make connections between ideas as they play.

How can we as practitioners make this happen for the children in our care?

Young children are curious by nature. They learn by exploring and experimenting and 'having a go'. As practitioners we need to provide a stimulating environment together with lots of opportunities and of course unlimited time! Although it can be a challenge in multi-purpose buildings, a creative environment can be created by leaving art materials and musical instruments out for children to play and experiment with.

Does there always need to be an 'end product' to creativity?

Practitioners and parents often both fall into the trap of only valuing an 'end product' as proof of creativity. How many of us have heard an anxious parent berating their young child with the words, 'have you made me a painting this morning Tom?' Children sometimes learn to rush to the painting easel and apply a few hurried strokes of paint to appease their carer, even though they may have been involved all morning playing imaginatively and creatively in the role-play area. We need to appreciate creative play and processes as just as important as any finished artwork!

What is the value of creative group work?

In many settings, children often work together to produce joint artwork and models, as well as singing, drama, dance and music performances. This can be seemingly problematic, as at times the individual creative process may have to be subordinated to the purpose and will of the group. However, group creative work can provide an ideal opportunity to develop children's social and co-operative skills. More often than not it requires more imagination and creativity to work as a group!

What can practitioners do to develop children's creativity?

You may now be feeling how do I encourage children in my care to develop their creativity? The following are useful hints for nurturing young children's creativity:

- Provide sufficient time and opportunities for children to explore, experiment and practice their skills. Allow children time to work at their own speed. Try to avoid them being pressured by other children eager to try another activity.
- Some children require more encouragement to 'have a go' on their own. They may need you to suggest ideas, stimulate their imagination, and encourage them. Children will discover a lot through their own explorations, but unless there is an adult on hand to talk about their discoveries, learning opportunities can be missed.
- Children need to feel secure. They need to know that help is available if and when they need it. The tricky job is judging when to intervene if a child is struggling. Sometimes the process of problem-solving is part of the learning process, but do be prepared to model and teach new skills that children may require in order to progress. Experience will help you maintain the balance between being intrusive, and avoiding the frustration children feel when their own efforts are thwarted.
- Supply good quality resources – both materials and people! Challenge children by inviting artists or performers to show children their own particular area of creativity. In particular make use of talented parents who are willing to help.
- Encourage children to talk to each other about their work. Ask them to share how they overcame problems when constructing a model robot, or why they decided to make a loud sound at the end of the music.
- Try to be creative yourself! How long is it since you found time to develop your own creative gifts? Challenge yourself to learn a new skill this year.

Exploring Stories, Songs and Rhymes

Creative Development is one of the six areas of learning in the Early Years Foundation Stage - the curriculum for all children under the age of five. The Statutory Framework published in 2007 breaks down Creative Development into four aspects. In this book each aspect is given its own logo, which you can find in the stories section of each topic.

The Four Aspects of Creative Development:

Being Creative – Responding to Experiences, Expressing and Communicating Ideas

Corresponding E.L.G.: Respond in a variety of ways to what they see, hear, smell, touch or feel.

Corresponding E.L.G.: Express and communicate their ideas, thoughts and feelings by using a widening range of materials, suitable tools, imaginative and role-play, movement, designing and making, and a variety of songs and musical instruments.

Exploring Media and Materials

Corresponding E.L.G.: Explore colour, texture, shape, form and space in two and three dimensions.

Creating Music and Dance

Corresponding E.L.G.: Recognise and explore how sounds can be changed, sing simple songs from memory, recognise repeated sounds and sound patterns and match movements to music.

Developing Imagination and Imaginative Play

Corresponding E.L.G.: Use their imagination in art and design, music, dance, imaginative and role-play and stories.

Stories, Songs and Rhymes

Stories

Stories can be used as a tool for creative development by providing a stimulus for work in all sorts of media. Hearing and using the language of stories also encourages children to use that language in their role-play.

Using the stories in this book

This book suggests a wealth of stories to read with children in the early years, these vary from traditional tales to modern picture books and even original stories, written especially for this book. Each story comes with a suggested creative activity designed to allow children to explore elements of the story further. Each of these activities is linked with one of the four aspects of Creative Development.

Songs

Singing is one of the earliest forms of creative expression and children are exposed to it even before they are born. Many mothers instinctively croon to their unborn child or small baby. As children develop language they will begin to express themselves vocally and through song. Singing in a group is at the beginning of musical life for all of us. The songs in this book are easy to learn as the majority are set to well-known tunes from nursery rhymes or traditional songs. The few original songs featured in this book are provided with notation in case you are feeling brave.

Rhymes

Recognising rhyme is a crucial part of developing creative listening skills, leading to an understanding of the patterns involved in words and music. The use of rhyme clearly overlaps with the Early Learning Goals for Communication, Language and Literacy, as learning songs and rhymes from memory is a vital part of learning to read. The rhymes in this book vary between finger and action rhymes through to poems and even raps.

Using the songs and rhymes in this book

Each song or rhyme in this book offers various possibilities for children to further develop their creative abilities. There are traditional songs and rhymes, variations on these, as well as brand new songs and rhymes.

In order to encourage as much creative play as possible, below are some suggestions for adapting each song or rhyme. At first these are likely to be led by the practitioner, but as children become used to experimenting with songs, rhythm and movement they will become confident in making up their own versions.

- Enjoy suggesting simple actions for children to copy and encourage children to create their own movements.
- Encourage movement to the rhythm and 'marching out' the beat.
- Suggest variations to the verse and ask children to come up with their own alternatives. For example "What are you wearing today/My coat and hat, coat and hat", "What are you wearing today/My scarf and gloves, scarf and gloves".

There are of course many other uses for the wealth of stories, songs and rhymes contained within this book, and it is hoped that the design of the book will allow each practitioner to adapt these to their individual teaching style.

Animals

Stories

The Gruffalo by Julia Donaldson
Design your own scary monster masks.

Rumble in the Jungle by Giles Andreae
Enjoy reciting poems and adding animal sound effects.

Noah's Ark Traditional
Give each child a partner and create a dance of pairs
of animals going on and off the ark.

The Leopard's Drum by Jessica Souhami
Act out the story, moving like the different animals
from the story.

Songs and rhymes

- Old Macdonald Had A Farm
- I Went To The Animal Fair
- Who Built The Ark?
- Baa Baa Black Sheep
- One Grey Elephant Balancing
- An Elephant Goes Like This And That
- The Animals Went In Two By Two
- Daddy's Taking Me To The Zoo Tomorrow
- The Lion And The Unicorn

Old Macdonald Had A Zoo
(Tune: Old Macdonald Had A Farm)
Old MacDonald had a zoo
E I E I O
And in that zoo there was a lion
E I E I O
With a roar, roar here
And a roar, roar there
Here a roar, there a roar
Everywhere a roar, roar,
Old MacDonald had a zoo
E I E I O
*What animals would you find in Old MacDonald's safari park/
petshop/pond/lake etc.?*

Walking Through The Jungle
Walking through the jungle
What do I see?
I can see a tiger looking at me.
Walking through the jungle
What do I hear?
I can hear a parrot squawk very near.

Walking through the jungle
What do I feel?
I can feel spider webs silvery and real.

I'm A Stripey Tiger
(Tune: I'm A Little Teapot)
I'm a stripey tiger, orange and black
See my stripes go down my back.
When I'm in the jungle, hear me roar
Then I sleep and start to snore!

Autumn

Stories

Autumn Is For Apples by Michelle Knudsen
Use Modroc and newspaper to create model apples.
Paint them different shades of yellow, green and red.

Autumn by Gerda Muller
Make plum jam or apple crumble and share at
snacktime.

Squirrel Nutkin by Beatrix Potter
Act out the story and learn the cheeky rhymes that
Squirrel Nutkin sings to old Mr Brown.

Pumpkin Soup by Helen Cooper
Act out the story as the animals make the soup
together, fall out, and then make friends again. Try
making some pumpkin soup and carve a pumpkin
lantern for Halloween.

Songs and rhymes

- Rolypoly Pudding And Blackberry Pie
- Five Little Leaves So Bright And Gay
- Here Is The Tree With Leaves So Green

Can You Catch a Red One?
(Tune: I Can Sing A Rainbow)
Red and orange and yellow and brown,
All the leaves falling around.
Can you catch a red one,
Catch a red one,
Catch a red one now?
(Then change colours...)

Firework Fingers
Five thin rockets standing tall
Leaning against the garden wall
One went pop
One went bang
One went fizz
One went clang
One went nowhere
And that left none at all.
(Countdown with fingers)

Autumn Memories
Apple peel and pumpkin pie
Golden leaves floating by
Blustery winds and bonfire burning
Prickly conker cases turning
Spiders spin, ghosts grin
Fireworks flash, raindrops splash
Misty Autumn morning here.

Bears

Stories

We're Going on a Bear Hunt by Michael Rosen
Chant the words of the rhyme and add actions
and sound effects using musical instruments.

Goldilocks and the Three Bears Traditional
Act out the story. What happens when the three bears
return to the house and find the intruder?

This Is The Bear by Sarah Hayes
Make annotated posters of Bear's adventures.

Where's My Teddy? by Jez Alborough
Draw spot the teddy pictures using ICT.

Songs and rhymes

- When Goldilocks Went To The House Of The Bears
- The Bear Went Over The Mountain
- Teddy Bear, Teddy Bear, Touch Your Nose
- The Teddy Bears' Picnic
- Round And Round The Garden Like A Teddy Bear

Hug Your Teddy Bear
(Tune: Wind The Bobbin' Up)
Hug your teddy bear,
Hug your teddy bear,
Hug, hug, hold him tight.
Smile if you love him,
Smile if you care,
Smile if you love your teddy bear.

Teddy Bear
(Tune: Tommy Thumb)
Teddy bear, teddy bear,
Where are you?
There you are, there you are,
How do you do.
(Repeat with other bears e.g. Polar bear, Grizzly bear, Panda bear, Koala bear etc.)

Teddy Is His Name-O
(Tune: Bingo Was His Name-o)
I have a teddy, I love him and Teddy is his name-o.
T E D D Y, T E D D Y, T E D D Y
And Teddy is his name-o.

Three Bears Dancing On The Beat
(Original tune)

There were three bears dancing on the beat. X3
Dancing down the street.

Daddy bear was dancing on the beat (loud)
Mummy bear was dancing on the beat (medium)
Baby bear was dancing on the beat (quiet)
Dancing down the street.

Change to marching, jumping, hopping, skipping, creeping, etc.

Clothes

Stories

The Elves and the Shoemaker Traditional
Make moving puppets for the elves from cardboard
shapes and split pins.
Act out the story using children and puppets.

Cinderella Traditional
Draw designs for Cinderella's rags and ballgown.

Mrs Lather's Laundry by Allan Ahlberg
Sing the washing song below.

Little Robin Red Vest by Jan Fearnley
Act out the story as Robin gives away his seven
vests to all his friends to help them keep warm.

Songs and rhymes

- Dingle-Dangle Scarecrow
- My Hat It Has Three Corners
- Down In The Jungle
- Cobbler Cobbler

Washing Song
(Tune: Here We Go Round The Mulberry Bush)
This is the way we wash the clothes,
Wash the clothes, wash the clothes.
This is the way we wash the clothes,
In the washing machine.

Watch them whirling round and round,
Round and round, round and round,
Watch them whirling round and round,
In the washing machine.

I can...
(Tune: Polly Put The Kettle On)
I can put my coat on X3
And do the buttons too.

I can tie my shoes up X3
Can I help you?

What Are You Wearing Today?
(Tune: Hickory Dickory Dock)
What are you wearing today?
What are you wearing today?
My coat and hat, coat and hat,

That's what I'm wearing today.
Try other pairs of clothes

Clothes Rhyme
Coats and shirts,
Trousers and skirts,
All my clothes are shrinking!
Shoes and tops,
Jumpers and socks,
But instead I'm thinking,
There's no way of knowing.
Perhaps it's me that's growing?

Colours

Stories

Little Red Riding Hood Traditional
Act out the story wearing the red cape.
Have fun pretending to be the wolf.

The Mixed-Up Chameleon by Eric Carle
Cut or tear out paper from a magazine and ask
children to design their own chameleons.

Little Robin Red Vest by Jan Fearnley
Create a dance for all the animals wearing Robin's
different coloured vests

The Rainbow Fish by Marcus Pfister
Paint pictures of rainbow fishes with one shiny
scale each.

Songs and rhymes

- I Can Sing A Rainbow
- Lavender's Blue
- Little Boy Blue
- In And Out The Dusky Bluebells

What's Your Favourite Colour?
(Tune: One Man Went To Mow)
Play this game with me,
What's your favourite colour?
Play this game, what's the same
As your favourite colour?
Red: tomatoes, apples, fire engines, ladybirds, peppers, poppies.

Stepping Stones to Creativity

Dilly Dilly

(Tune: Lavender's Blue)

Daffodils are yellow
Dilly dilly
Roses are red.
Cornflowers are blue
Dilly dilly
In my flower bed.

Apples are green
Dilly dilly
Strawberries are red
Bananas are yellow
Dilly dilly
Now you are fed.

Emeralds are green
Dilly dilly
Sapphires are blue.
Rubies are red
Dilly dilly,
Rich stones for you.

Spotting Colours

Hop for yellow
Stretch for blue
Spotting colours, one and two.
Shout for orange
Sit for brown
Look for colours all around.
Wink for pink
Whisper for white
Lots of colours, what a sight!
Jump for red
Crouch for green
How many colours have you seen?

Dinosaurs

Stories

 Tyrannosaurus Drip by Julia Donaldson
Make model dinosaurs out of salt and flour dough
or clay. Paint the models in bright colours.

 Bumpus Jumpus Dinosaurumpus by Tony Mitton
Have fun reciting the rhyming text and add sound effects.

 The Dance of the Dinosaurs by Colin Hawkins
Create a dinosaur dance with the children.

 Harry and the Bucketful of Dinosaurs by Ian Whybrow
Act out the story using a plastic bucket and some
small toy dinosaurs.

Songs and rhymes

I Saw A Dinosaur

I thought I saw a dinosaur,
I thought I heard its mighty roar,
I thought I felt its sharp claw,
But do you know what is weird?
I really saw a dinosaur,
I really heard its mighty roar,
I really felt its sharp claw,
And then it disappeared!

Five Fierce Dinosaurs

(Tune: Ten Green Bottles)

Five fierce dinosaurs standing in a row X2
And if one fierce dinosaur should flick his tail and go
There'd be four fierce dinosaurs standing in a row…

Dina The Dinosaur

(Tune: Hey Diddle Diddle)

Dina the dinosaur
Sat on the river floor
And dined on dinner at ten
She ate some fish
From a silvery dish
And then ran back home again.

Dina the dinosaur
Opened her giant jaw
Then began to roar
She lay down to rest
In a cosy nest
And soon began to snore.

Families

Stories

 Dr. Xargle's Book of Earthlets by Jeanne Willis
Design and paint an alien family.

 Big Book of Families by Catherine Anholt
Paint a portrait of your own family from a photograph.

 Tell Me What It's Like To Be Big by Joyce Dunbar
Act out Willa's attempts to 'do things for herself'.

 Grandad Pot by Siobhan Dodds
Act out the story as Grandad cooks lots of food for
Polly and her friends.

Songs and rhymes

- Here Are Grandma's Glasses
- There Were Ten In The Bed
- Tommy Thumb
- Jack Sprat
- There Was An Old Woman Who Lived In A Shoe
- Rock-A-Bye Baby

The Family's In The Ring

(Tune: Farmers In His Den)
The family's in the ring
The family's in the ring
E I E I
The family's in the ring.

The father wants a wife…
The wife wants a child…
The child wants a sister/brother…

In My Family

(Tune: Oh My Darling)
In my family, in my family,
There are three of us you see.
Mum and dad, mum and dad,
And me makes three.
Plus my sister, plus my sister,
Altogether that makes four.
And my nana, and my nana,
No there are not any more.
In my family, in my family,
There are five of us you know.
Wait a minute, wait a minute,
Should I count the baby too?

Farms

Stories

 The Enormous Turnip Traditional
Act out the story as the farmer, his family and lots of
animals try to lift the turnip. Add sound effects.

 Farmer Duck by Martin Waddell
Act out the story with all the animals doing the work.

 *The Pig in the Pond* by Martin Waddell
Collect together paintings or drawings of all the
different farm animals and mount them into a large
group collage with scrunched up cling film and
plastic for the water.

 The Little Red Hen Traditional
Make some bread and sing the song on the following
page.

Songs and rhymes

- I Went To Visit A Farm One Day
- Old Macdonald Had A Farm
- Baa Baa Black Sheep
- The Farmer's In His Dell
- One Man Went To Mow
- Oat And Beans And Barley Grow

Ten Little Piglets On The Farm

(Tune: Ten Little Indians)
There was one, there were two
There were three little piglets
There were four, there were five
There were six little piglets,
There were seven, there were eight,
There were nine little piglets
Ten little piglets on the farm.

Repeat with different animals

Down On The Farm.

(Tune: The Wheels On The Bus)
The cows in the barn say moo, moo, moo
Moo, moo, moo, moo, moo, moo
The cows in the barn say moo, moo, moo
Down on the farm.

Try with different farm animals

Little Hen Wants To Make Some Bread
(Tune: Here We Go Round The Mulberry Bush)
Little hen wants to make some bread,
Make some bread, make some bread.
Little hen wants to make some bread.
Poor little red hen.

This is the way she plants the seed...
This is the way she grinds the corn...
This is the way she bakes the bread...
Little red hen won't share the bread...

Flight
Stories

Pigs Might Fly by Jonathan Emmett
Design and build model planes from recycled
materials for the three little pigs.

Kite Flying by Grace Lin
Make up a kite dance, making stretching and curling
body shapes to floaty music.

The Firebird Traditional
Design a collage picture of a firebird using feathers,
paint, sequins, and sparkly materials.

Amazing Airplanes by Tony Mitton
Make a wall display of a giant plane with a window
showing each child's face.

The Owl Babies by Martin Waddell
Act out the story and learn the 'Three Little Owls'
Rhyme.

Songs and rhymes

- Two Little Dicky Birds
- Five Little Ducks Went Swimming One Day

Oh When The Plane
(Tune: Oh When The Saints)
Oh when the plane
Goes flying by
Oh when the plane
Goes flying by
I want to be in that airplane
As it flies high in the sky.

My Airplane
(Tune: My Bonnie)
The aeroplane flies over the ocean
The aeroplane flies over the sea
The aeroplane flies back to the airport
And brings back my home to me.

Five Fat Blackbirds
(Tune: Ten Green Bottles)
Five fat blackbirds sitting in a tree
Five fat blackbirds sitting in a tree
And if one fat blackbird should fly away free
There'd be four fat blackbirds sitting in a tree.

Three Little Owls
Three little owls in a nest in a tree
Are very, very hungry, as hungry as can be.
Mother owl goes hunting, at night goes she.
Three little owls in a nest in a tree.

Three little owls in a nest in a tree
Missing their mother, as lonely as can be.
Mother owl returns with food for all three.
Three little owls in a nest in a tree.

Food

Stories

The Tiger Who Came to Tea by Judith Kerr
Paint big pictures of the tiger and all the food he ate.

Pumpkin Soup by Helen Cooper
Make some vegetable soup with the children to share at snack time. Act out the story as you stir and season the soup.

I Will Not Ever Never Eat A Tomato by Lauren Child
Act out situations where children refuse to eat different food.

Biscuit Bear by Mini Grey
Write and illustrate new stories about the adventures of Biscuit Bear.

The Lighthouse Keeper's Lunch by Ronda Armitage
Get children to design their own 3D model of a favourite picnic lunch.

Songs and rhymes

- I Like To Eat…
- Food Glorious Food
- Five Currant Buns
- Five Fat Sausages
- Five Fat Peas
- One Potato
- Jelly On The Plate
- Hot Cross Buns
- Polly Put The Kettle On
- Old Tom Tomato
- Pease Pudding Hot
- Pat-A-Cake
- Curly Locks
- Jack Sprat
- Little Jack Horner
- Do You Know The Muffin Man?

Eat Vegetables
(Tune: Aram Sam Sam)
Eat vegetables, eat vegetables,
Eat carrots, peas and broccoli, eat vegetables
Eat vegetables, eat vegetables,
Eat carrots, peas and broccoli, eat vegetables.
Be healthy, be healthy,
Eat carrots, peas and broccoli, eat vegetables.

Be healthy, be healthy,
Eat carrots, peas and broccoli, eat vegetables.

Sandwiches
(Tune: Did You Ever See A Lassie?)
Would you like to make a sandwich,
A sandwich, a sandwich?
Would you like to make a sandwich,
A sandwich with me?
Put some cheese in your sandwich,
Your sandwich, your sandwich.
Put some cheese in your sandwich,
Cheese sandwich for tea.

Change the fillings…

Friends

Stories

Lost And Found by Oliver Jeffers
Draw or paint a portrait of your best friend.

Sharing Shell by Julia Donaldson
Create a 3D collage wall display of life in the rock pool with all the different colourful creatures.

Mabel's Magical Garden by Paula Metcalf
Paint comparative pictures of the garden at the beginning of the story and then the garden deprived of sunshine.

The Ugly Duckling Traditional
Act out scenes from the story.

Stepping Stones to Creativity

Songs and rhymes

- Polly Put The Kettle On
- Girls And Boys Come Out To Play

Greeting Rhyme

Two best friends, met in a lane,
Hugged each other, and then hugged again,
Said, 'How are you,'
'How are you,'
And 'how are you' again?

Bend thumbs over to greet each other.

My Friend And I

(Tune: Lavender's Blue)
My friend and I
(dilly dilly)
We like to play.
My friend and I
(dilly dilly)
Play all the day

My friend and I
(dilly dilly)
We like to share.
My friend and I
(dilly dilly)
Share cos we care/
Sharing my bear

Making Friends

(Tune: Kumbayah)
Come and share with me
Making friends
Come and share with me
Making friends
Come and share with me
Making friends
Oh _____, be my friend.

Insert name of friend in the gap.

Come and play/read/skip/
swim/eat/etc. with me…

Let's not quarrel now,
Be my friend,
Let's not quarrel now,
Be my friend,
Let's not quarrel now,
Be my friend.
Oh _____, be my friend.

Gardens

Stories

Jasper's Beanstalk by Nick Butterworth
Use either a days of the week rhyme such as 'Solomon Grundy' or use rhymes below to create your own rhyme about Jasper's attempts to grow a plant.

Oliver's Vegetables by Vivian French
Act out the story as Oliver learns to try different vegetables from granddad's garden.

Eddie's Garden by Sarah Garland
Use ICT, draw or paint a design of your own garden.

The Global Garden by Kate Petty
Create a visual aid using flaps and wheels from the book to share information about plants from around the world.

Songs and rhymes

- I Went to the Garden and Dug up the Ground
- Mary Mary Quite Contrary
- Sing a Song of Sixpence

The Vegetables are Growing

(Tune: John Brown's body)
The vegetables are growing
In my garden, in a line.
The vegetables are growing
In my garden, now it's fine.
The vegetables are growing
In my garden, all the time.
Let's count them carefully.
Can you count the orange carrots?
Can you count the tasty spinach?
Can you count the new potatoes?
Growing in the ground.

A Week In The Garden

On Monday I planted the seed.
On Tuesday I pulled out a weed.
On Wednesday I watered the ground.
On Thursday I walked all around.
On Friday I began to doubt.
On Saturday I pulled the seed out!
On Sunday I did what I do best.
Sat in my garden having a rest!

Growth

Stories

Jack and the Beanstalk Traditional
Explore pitch, i.e. high and low sounds, using a xylophone or keyboard. Increase the pitch as the beanstalk grows taller.

The Tiny Seed by Eric Carle
Copy the book's unique style of art by tearing paper of different colours to create a collage of flowers.

The Enormous Turnip Traditional
Act out the story.

Once there were Giants by Martin Waddell
Draw a picture of what each child wants to be when grown up.

Songs and rhymes

- Mary Mary Quite Contrary
- I Went To The Garden And Dug Up The Ground
- Five Fat Peas In A Peapod Pressed
- 'Now I Am Six' by A.A.Milne
- Oats And Beans And Barley Grow
- I Had A Little Nut Tree
- Once I Found A Cherry Stone

I Grow Best While I'm Asleep

I grow best while I'm asleep,
Out from the covers my toes will peep.
My hair will grow, my fingers too,
I'm still growing, how about you?

And That's Not All!

When I was a baby
I couldn't even walk.
When I was a baby
I couldn't even talk.
Now I am five
I've grown very tall.
I can run and skip and jump
And that's not all!
I can sing and shout out loud
And that's not all!
I can read and write my name
And that's not all!

(Add own achievements?)

Down In The Garden

(Tune: Down In The Jungle)
Down in the garden
Where nobody goes,
I planted a seed
To watch it grow.
I watered it here,
I watered it there,
I watered it just about everywhere!

It grew very, very tall
It grew very, very tall
It grew very, very tall
It grew just about everywhere!

Holes

Stories

Peepo! by Janet and Allan Ahlberg
Paint or draw a picture of a baby's or child's activities and then place a piece of paper on top with a hole cut out in the style of the book.

Another Fine Mess by Tony Bonning
Use junk materials and empty food packets to create pictures from the story.

Wait Until Dinnertime by Mel Astill
Add sound effects to the story below using voices, body percussion and musical instruments.

Wait until Dinnertime

Baby Rabbit was hungry. "You're always hungry", said Mummy Rabbit, "wait until dinnertime!" Baby Rabbit leapt out of his burrow hole. "Mmmm", he thought, "what can I eat?" He hopped into the next burrow hole and found some delicious carrots that Grandad Rabbit was saving for breakfast. "Mmmm, crunchy", he said as he munched.

Baby Rabbit climbed through the next burrow hole and found some crisp, green lettuce leaves that Uncle Rabbit was saving for lunch. "Mmmm, lovely", he said as he munched.

Baby Rabbit squeezed into the next burrow hole and found some fresh dandelions that cousin rabbit was saving for dinner. "Mmmm, tasty", he said as he munched.

Baby Rabbit felt rather full and tired after all that eating. He peered out of the burrow hole, it was getting dark. "Dinnertime", he could hear Mummy Rabbit calling. "I must get back to my burrow," he said. But oh dear, Baby Rabbit was stuck. His tummy

was too big and too full and the hole was too small. He pushed and squeezed but it was no good.

"Mummy, I'm stuck!" he cried. Mummy Rabbit took his paws and heaved and pulled and eventually out popped Baby Rabbit. "Next time I think you should wait until dinnertime!" said mummy.

Songs and rhymes

- There's A Hole In My Bucket
- Put Your Finger In Foxy's Hole

Make Me A Doughnut
(Tune: Pat-A-Cake)
Pat-a-cake, pat-a-cake, baker's man,
Bake me a doughnut, as fast as you can.
Mix it and shape it, and roll in a ring,
Make me a doughnut that's fit for a king!

Make A Hole
(Tune: Oh We Can Play On The Big Bass Drum)
Can you make a hole with your fingers?
And this is the way you do it.
Make a hole with your fingers and thumb
And then you can look right through it.

Can you make a hole with both your hands?
And this is the way you do it.
Join your fingers and join your thumbs
And then you can look right through it.

Holidays

Stories

Mr Bear's Holiday by Debi Gliori
Design a fancy patterned tent to rival Mr. Bear's.

Lisa's Airplane Trip by Anne Gutman
Act out Lisa's adventures on her first experience on a plane.

The Cat Who Wanted To Go Home by Jill Tomlinson
Use balloons, papier mache and paint to create model hot-air balloons.

Holiday Day by Mel Astill
Paint a picture of a perfect holiday day.

Holiday Day

Martha wanted to go on holiday. On a holiday with sun for bathing in, waves for splashing in, sand for building with and lots of ice cream for licking. But…. mum and dad were always busy at work and that meant no holiday for Martha.

One Saturday, Martha woke up, and discovered it was sunny and hot, the perfect day for a holiday. "Oh I wish I had waves to splash in, sand to build with and even just one ice-cream to lick would be nice," thought Martha. She went downstairs to have breakfast. Where were mum and dad? Busy as usual, thought Martha grumpily.

She called out, no answer. She called again and listened…. she could hear laughing and splashing sounds in the garden. Martha ran outside. Mum and dad had been busy. The paddling pool was full with cool, sparkling water. The sand pit was full with bright yellow sand for building castles, and there was even a beach towel for bathing in the sun. It WAS going to be the most perfect holiday day!

"Now then," said mum, "time for breakfast! What will it be: toast, cornflakes, porridge or….an ice cream for licking?"

Can you guess what Martha chose?

Songs and rhymes

- We're all going on a summer holiday

On my holiday
(Tune: Jelly on the plate)
On my holiday
On my holiday
Building castles
Building castles
Lots of games to play.

On my holiday
On my holiday
Fill the bucket
Fill the bucket
Lots of games
to play.

Other verses could include these choruses: turn it over, hoist the flag, have a paddle, waves are coming, now the castle's gone!

Houses and Homes

Stories

 The Three Little Pigs Traditional
Act out the story.

 The Three Liitle Wolves And The Big Bad Pig by Eugene Trivizas
Use a range of materials to create a model-house that the three little pigs couldn't demolish!

 Hansel and Gretel Tradtional
Create a giant collage picture of a house made of all the children's favourite sweets using wrappers and labels.

 The Little, Little House by Jessica Souhami
Cut paper shapes in the style of the artwork to create a picture of a house bursting at the seams.

Songs and rhymes

- I'm Going To Build A Little House
- How many people live in your house?
- This Is The House That Jack Built
- Peter Hammers With One Hammer
- There Was A Crooked Man
- To Market, To Market

Made Into A Home

(Tune: The Wheels On The Bus)
My house is built of big red bricks,
Big red bricks, big red bricks,
My house is built of big red bricks,
Made into a home.

My house is built with four wide windows,
Four wide windows, four wide windows,
My house is built with four wide windows,
Made into a home.

Make up new verses using these ideas: a tiled roof, a 'red' front door, a garden wall, a long green garage etc.

Jason Builds

(Tune; Peter Hammers)
Jason builds with one brick,
One brick, one brick.
Jason builds with one brick
All day long.
Sally builds with two bricks…

Build up the rhyme using the names of all children, then count back down again.

Journeys

Stories

 The Train Ride by June Crebbin
Recite the story rhythmically as a chant and add sound effects for the different things the train passes on its journey.

 We All Go Traveling By by Sheena Roberts
Sing along to the accompanying CD and have fun creating sound effects.

 The Snail and the Whale by Julia Donaldson
Draw and paint pictures of maps of the snail's journey.

 Hansel and Gretel Traditional
Act out the story of the children's journey through the forest, following a trail.

Songs and rhymes

- The Wheels On The Bus
- Row Row Row The Boat
- Ride A Cock Horse

Visiting

(Tune: I went to visit a farm one day)
We went to visit the/a _____ one day
We'll see a _____ along the way
What d'ya think we'll hear it say?

Fill in the gaps with appropriate words such as friend/house/shop/ farm/park/zoo/sea etc.

Travelling Rap

(Echo each line)
Open the gate
Don't be late
Get in the car
Don't go far
Down the road
Watch the load

Round the bend
Towards the end
Going fast
Can't be last
Slowing down
Into town
Come to a stop
That's your lot!

I'm On A Journey
(Tune: Ants go marching)
My feet go marching two by two, Hurrah, hurrah,
My feet go marching two by two,
Hurrah, hurrah,
My feet go marching two by two,
They're marching round to come see you
And I'm on a journey, traveling along.

My car is driving very fast,
Hurrah, hurrah,
My car is driving very fast,
Hurrah, hurrah,
My car is driving very fast,
Its driving fast, it won't be last,
And I'm on a journey, traveling along.

The train is whizzing quickly by,
Hurrah, hurrah,
The train is whizzing quickly by,
Hurrah, hurrah,
The train is whizzing quickly by,
Look out the window as we fly,
And I'm on a journey, traveling along.

Light

Stories

By The Light Of The Moon by Sheridan Cain
Act out the story helping Little Mouse to find a new nest.

Lights Out! Shadow Pop-Up And Play by Richard Fowler
Make shadow pictures using hands, objects and torches, or other light sources. Then make outlines from black sugar paper to shine a light through.

How To Catch A Star by Oliver Jeffers
Try painting pictures using the original, bold watercolour style in the book.

Lighting A Lamp by Jonny Zucker
Make diva lamps for Divali using painted clay and tea lights.

Songs and rhymes

- Starlight, Starbright
- Twinkle, Twinkle Little Star
- Up The Tall White Candlestick

Five Fizzing Fireworks
Five fizzing fireworks,
(Hold up five fingers)
Sparkling high
(Wiggle fingers)
In the dark November sky.
One went bang!
(Clap hands)
And shone so bright,
(Make a big circle with hands)
Lighting up the cold, dark night.

Four fizzing fireworks…

Switch My Torch On
(Tune: Wind The Bobbin Up)
Switch my torch on
Switch my torch on
In the middle of the night.
Shine it on the ceiling.
Shine it on the floor.
Shine it on my face.
And shine it on the door.
When the door opens,
I quickly go quiet,
Dive under the duvet
And switch off the light.

Three Bright Lights
(Tune: Three Blind Mice)
Three bright lights
Three bright lights
Sun, stars and moon,
Sun, stars and moon,
They all light up the
sky so high
At different times of day
and night
Did you ever see such
a wonderful sight
As three bright lights?

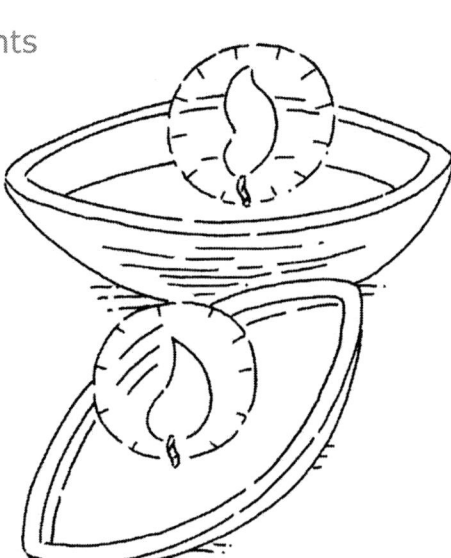

Machines

Stories

Duck in the Truck by Jez Alborough
Act out the story.

Amazing Machines by Tony Mitton
Use words from the book to create sound effects using vocal and body percussion or instruments.

Mole Machines by Judith Harries
Design and construct machines from a variety of materials.

Mole Machines

Farmer Huntley needed help. His tractor had broken down. "I need a new machine to dig up the potatoes" he said. "I shall give a reward to anyone who can invent a machine to help me." So he put up a poster advertising the competition all over the farm.

Carla Cow decided to have a go. She fixed together two wheels and a length of piping to make a machine, but it got stuck in the mud and a wheel fell off.

Harry Horse thought he could do better. He fixed together four wheels, a coat hanger and a spade to make a machine, but the spade snapped in half.

Felix Fox was very clever. He fixed together a ladder, a shovel and a battery to make a machine, but the rungs of the ladder were rotten and broke.

Monty Mole smiled to himself. He had a really good idea for a digging machine. And so, he sharpened his claws, polished his nose, and began to dig. Farmer Huntley and the other animals were all very impressed with Monty and decided that the best digging machine of all had in fact been right under their noses!

Songs and rhymes

- Down By The Station
- The Wheels On The Bus
- Hickory Dickory Dock

Robot, Robot Turn Around

(Tune: We Three Kings)
See my robot marching around
See my robot making a sound
Wheels-a-turning, cogs-a-whirring
Spinning on the ground.

Oh robot, robot turn around.
Robot, robot make a sound.
Left and right and up and down.
Robot, robot turn around.

The Wheels On My Machine

(Tune: The Wheels On The Bus)
The wheels on my machine go round and round
Round and round, round and round.
The wheels on my machine go round and round,
All day long.

The lights on my machine flash on and off…
The buttons on my machine switch up and down…

Materials

Stories

The Three Little Pigs Traditional
Make collage houses using different materials such as art straws; lolipop sticks and twigs; and printed Duplo bricks.

Stone Soup Traditional
Act out the story.

The Wooden Dragon by Joan Aiken
Use clay and other modeling material to create baby dragons.

Painted Pebbles by Judith Harries
Try painting some pebbles.

Painted Pebbles

Adam loved painting. He painted all the time. At nursery he painted pictures at the easel. At home he painted pictures at the kitchen table. Mummy put them on the fridge or took them to work to brighten up her office. In the bathroom he painted on the tiles with special bath paints. In the garden he painted with water on the wall. In the holidays, at grandma's house, Adam painted her wooden chair. "Oh dear Adam! That was my favourite chair!" They scrubbed it with soapy water but the paint would not come off. Grandma sighed and then said "I have an idea; let's go down to the beach and find something to paint." Adam was confused. He couldn't think of anything he could paint at the beach.

Grandma walked along the shingle, away from her usual spot on the sand, and bent down to pick up stones. "That's a good one" she said, as she dropped a pebble into Adam's plastic bucket. Adam followed her up and down the beach but couldn't guess what she was planning.

Back in grandma's kitchen, she showed him how to paint the pebbles and turn them into different creatures. Adam painted with a big smile on his face. He knew that he would never run out of pebbles to paint.

Songs and rhymes

● Peter Hammers With One Hammer
● There's A Hole In My Bucket
● London Bridge Is Falling Down
● Humpty Dumpty

Materials
(Tune: My Hat It Has Three Corners)
My hat is made of felt,
My scarf is made of wool,
My gloves are made of leather,
And they all keep me warm.
My house is made of bricks,
My roof is made of tiles,
My windows are made of glass,
And they all make my home.

The triangle is made of metal
The claves are made of wood
The castanets are made of plastic
And they all make good sounds.

Minibeasts

Stories

The Very Hungry Caterpillar by Eric Carle
Look at the changes in the book from an egg to a caterpillar, a pupa to a butterfly and make a lifecycle wheel.

The Bad-Tempered Ladybird by Eric Carle
Talk about and act out the change in the ladybird as it meets the different animals in the story.

Anansi The Spider Traditional Caribbean
Make model spiders from egg-boxes and pipe cleaners.

Tadpole's Promise by Jeanne Willis
Use brightly coloured felt or sweet -wrappers to create collages of rainbow caterpillars.

Songs and rhymes

● There's A Worm At The Bottom Of My Garden
● Little Arabella Miller
● Incy Wincy Spider
● Little Miss Muffet
● There Was An Old Woman Who Swallowed A Fly

What A Lot Of Bugs
(Finger rhyme)
Buzzing bees, flying flies,
Darting dragonflies.
Wiggling worms, spinning spiders,
Crawling caterpillars.
Slow snails, lazy ladybirds,
Silly centipedes.
Bustling beetles, slithering slugs,
What a lot of bugs!

A Very Hungry Caterpillar
(Tune: original)

A very hungry caterpillar sat upon a leaf,
Munch, munch, munch, munch, munch, munch, munch.
A very hungry caterpillar sat upon a leaf,
Munch, munch, munch, munch eating his lunch.

The caterpillar got much fatter and he span around.
Spin, spin, spin, spin, spin, spin, spin.
The caterpillar got much fatter and he span around.
Spin, spin, spin, spin. Like a pin.

A dry and brown pupa case fell upon the ground.
There it lay without a sound.
A dry and brown pupa case fell upon the ground.
There it lay without a sound.

A rainbow-coloured butterfly flew into the air.
Flap, flap, flap, flap, flap, flap, flap.
A rainbow-coloured butterfly flew into the air.
Flap, flap, flap, flap, flap, flap, flap.

Night

Stories

 Night Monkey, Day Monkey by Julia Donaldson
Paint contrasting pictures of night and day.

 Can't You Sleep, Little Bear? by Martin Waddell
Act out the story as Little Bear struggles to sleep
and Big Bear helps him not to be afraid of the dark.

 Peace At Last by Jill Murphy
Use musical instruments to create sound effects for
all the sounds of the night that keep Mr. Bear awake.

 The Baby Who Wouldn't Go To Bed by Helen Cooper
Act out the story of the baby driving around in his
red car to avoid going to bed!

Songs and rhymes

- Diddle Diddle Dumpling
- Twinkle Twinkle Little Star
- Golden Slumbers

One Dark Dark Night
(Tune: original)

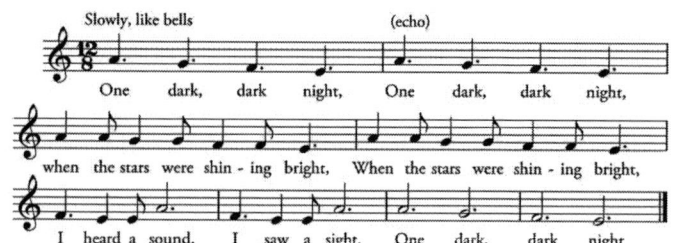

One dark dark night
When the stars were shining bright
I heard a sound
I saw a sight
One dark dark night.

One dark dark night
When the stars were shining bright
I felt a touch
I had a fright
One dark dark night.

Numbers

Stories

 Handa's Surprise by Eileen Browne
Create a series of paintings and collages to show the
fruit bowl as the fruit gradually disappears.

 Snow White and the seven dwarfs Traditional
Paint portraits of different dwarves, then label each
one, frame and display.

 Three Billy Goat's Gruff Traditional
Use three different sized toy goats to act out and retell
the story. Ask children to design a really scary troll
mask and then use in their drama.

 One Hundred Hungry Ants by Elinor Pinczes
Use pen and ink to create numbers made from ants.

Songs and rhymes

- Five Fat Sausages
- Five Fat Peas In A Peapod Pressed
- Five Currant Buns
- 12345, Once I Caught A Fish Alive
- When I Was One I Ate A Bun
- Five Little Ducks

- Ten Green Bottles
- Going to St. Ives
- Hickory Dickory Dock

I Am Five Years Old Today

I am five years old today.
I am no longer four.
I'm feeling very grown up
And I can tell you more.
That now I'm five,
There's just one thing
I really want for me.
To be six years old,
And that's not all,
As quickly as can be!

Five Bright Candles

Five bright candles on a birthday cake.
1, 2, 345, there's really no mistake.
Take a big breath and away we go!
Out go the candles as we blow!

I Like To Count

(Tune: Bingo)
I like to count, there is no doubt
And counting is my game-o
1, 2, 345, 1, 2, 345, 1, 2, 345,
And counting is my game-o.

I like to count, there is no doubt
And counting is my game-o
6, 7, 8 9 10, 6, 7, 8 9 10, 6, 7, 8 9 10
And counting is my game-o.

I like to count, there is no doubt
I like counting backwards
10, 9, 876, 5,4,321, now there are no more
And counting is my game-o.

Opposites

Stories

Opposites by Nick Butterworth
Draw and paint pictures of opposites on folded
sugar paper.

The Little Red Ant and the Great Big Crumb
by Shirley Climo
Act out the story as little red ant tries to move the
big crumb.

Mary Mary Quite Contrary by Judith Harries
Act out the story. Can the children think of any more
opposites for Mary to try?

Mary Mary Quite Contrary

Mary was very contrary.

*When mum said, "please can you fetch me a big plate?", Mary did
the opposite and brought a small one!*

*When mum said, "please be quiet Mary, your baby sister is asleep,"
Mary did the opposite and made lots of noise!*

*When dad said, "Mary, we must walk to school quickly to meet your
brother," Mary did the opposite and walked really slowly!
Mum would sigh and say "Mary Mary quite contrary!" and then
one day they made a plan. That night mum and dad offered to
read Mary a really long bedtime story. Mary, as always, wanted the
opposite. Until she thought of all the tales she would be missing…*

Songs and rhymes

- Jack And Jill Went Up The Hill
- The Grand Old Duke of York
- Hickory Dickory Dock
- Goosey Goosey Gander

Opposites Song

(Tune: If You're Happy And You Know It)
If you're happy and you know it, clap your hands…
If you're sad and you know it, pull a face…
If you're hot and you know it, wipe your brow…
If you're cold and you know it, shiver alot…
If you're tall and you know it, touch the sky…
If you're short and you know it, touch the floor…

Opposites Rap

Big and small, short and tall, finding the opposites rap
High and low, fast and slow, end it with a clap.
Hot and cold, new and old, more of them we've found
Fat and thin, out and in, lots of them around
Happy and sad, good and bad, finding the opposites rap
Black and white, day and night, end it with a clap.

Ourselves

Stories

Funnybones by Allan Ahlberg
Cut and stick white art straws to create skeletons on black sugar paper.

We've All Got Belly Buttons by David Martin
Draw around a child's body on a large sheet of paper and paint on clothes and a face. Add labels for all the body parts from the book.

When An Elephant Comes To School by Jan Ormerod
Ask children to remember how they felt on their first day at school and act it out.

Rumpelstiltskin Traditional
Play a circle game with the children's names. Clap two times slowly, and then pause for two counts. Ask children to take turns around the circle to say or sing their name in the gap.

Songs and rhymes

- Heads, Shoulders, Knees And Toes
- One Finger, One Thumb, Keep Moving
- If You're Happy And You Know It
- Round And Round The Garden
- Oliver Twist, You Can't Do This

There's Lots of Bones In Me!
(Tune: There Are No Strings On Me from Pinnochio)
I've got two eyes, a mouth and nose,
Ten little fingers and ten little toes.
I've got two legs and two strong arms,
There's lots of bones in me!

I've got two hands, a neck and chin,
And lots of skin to keep them in.
I've got a spine, a skull and ribs,
There's lots of bones in me!

Tickling rhymes
(Tune: Round And Round The Garden)
Up and down the hillside
(Tickle up and down arms)
Run the naughty ants
Up and down, round and round
(Tickle up and down, round and round)
And into your pants.
(End with pat on the bottom)

Hello!
(Tune: Here I Come)

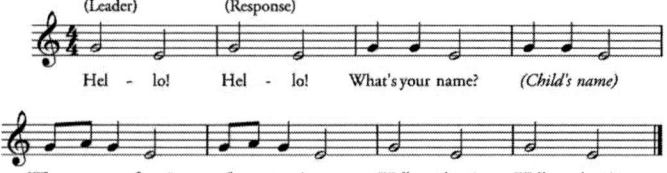

Leader	Response
Hello!	Hello
What's your name?	(insert child's name)
Where are you from?	(insert home town)
Well done!	Well done!
Bonjour	Bonjour
Guten Tag	Guten Tag
Say shalom	Say shalom
Well done!	Well done!

Patterns

Stories

My Mum And Dad Make Me Laugh by Nick Sharatt
Design spotty clothes for mum and stripey clothes for dad.

How The Leopard Got His Spots by Rudyard Kipling
Research and paint animal patterns.

Who Are You, Stripy Horse? by Jim Helmore
Create patterned and collage pictures in the style of the book.

A Bad Case Of Stripes by David Shannon
Get the children to make colourful stripey self-portraits of themselves.

Songs and rhymes

Patchwork Quilt
(Tune: This old man)
Patchwork quilt
Matching squares
Each one sewn together with care.
Stripes and flowers and rows of dots
What a lot of patterns we've got!

Patchwork quilt
Matching squares
Each one makes me want to stare
Red and yellow and orange too
Such a lot of patterns for you.

Let's Make A Pattern
(Tune: original)

Up and down, up and down, stretch and bend, stretch and bend,
Tall and small, Tall and small, Let's make a bo-dy pat-tern.

Up and down, up and down,
Stretch and bend, stretch and bend,
Tall and small, tall and small,
Let's make a body pattern.

Stamp and clap, stamp and clap,
Click and tap, click and tap,
Pop and slap, pop and slap,
Let's make a noisy pattern.

Pets

Stories

I Want A Pet by Lauren Child
Design your own perfect pet that nobody in the family will object to.

I Wish I Were A Dog by Lydia Monks
Use the vibrant colour illustrations to inspire children to paint pictures of their own pets.

I Want a Cat by Tony Ross
Act out the story

That Pesky Rat by Lauren Child
Use black sugar paper and coloured tissue paper to make a cityscape of buildings in the style of the book. Glue a cut-out rat in front of the cityscape.

Songs and rhymes

● Pussy Cat, Pussy Cat
● I Love Little Pussy

● Ding Dong Bell
● How Much Is That Doggie In The Window?

My Poorly Pet
(Tune: original)

My poor-ly pet needs to see the vet, My poor-ly pet needs to see the vet,
My poor-ly pet needs to see the vet, He has hurt his paw.

My poorly pet needs to see the vet X3
He has hurt his _____
Insert different parts of pet such as tail, leg, head, ear, fin, paw, etc.

Please Be My Pet
(Tune: Pease Pudding Hot)
Please be my pet
Sweet pussy cat
I will look after you
Fancy that!

Please be my pet
Fine puppy dog
I will look after you
Go for a jog!

Please be my pet
Brown guinea pig
I will look after you
Dance a jig!

Hippety Hop To The Pet Shop
(Tune: Hippety Hop to the Candy Shop)
Hippety hop to the pet shop
To buy a pet for Mary
Try a cat, perhaps a fish,
Or even a canary.

Hippety hop to the pet shop
To buy a pet for Peter.
Try a dog, perhaps a snake
Or better still a cheetah!

Try making up your own verses using children's names and different pets.

Pirates

Stories

 The Lighthouse Keeper's Breakfast by Ronda Armitage
Dress up as pirates and act out the story.

 The Night Pirates by Peter Harris
Cut out different papers to create pictures of the
pirate ship and houses in the style of the book.

 Tiny Ted and the Pirates by Ian Whybrow
Act out the story.

 Pirate Pete by Kim Kennedy
Draw an annotated treasure map.

 Captain Flinn and the Pirate Dinosaurs by Giles Andreae
Paint a picture of each child's favourite pirate dinosaur.

Songs and rhymes

● What Shall We Do With The Drunken Sailor?

We're Going On A Treasure Hunt
(Tune: We're Going On A Bear Hunt)
We're going on a treasure hunt,
We're going to find some treasure.
What a beautiful day.
We're not scared.
Uh oh!
Sinking sand!
We can't go over it
We can't go under it
We've got to go through it.
Squelch, squelch, squelch!
Sharp rough rocks – climb, trip, scratch…
Deep cold water – splash, splash, splash…
Dark damp cave – creep, creep, creep…
What's inside?
Is it the treasure?
It's got feathers and a sharp beak.
Screech, screech, screech…

Run to safety backwards through the rhyme.

Looking For Treasure
Looking for treasure
Searching for jewels
Reading the map
Following the rules
X marks the spot

Where treasure was hid
Stepping the trail
As the pirates did.

The Treasure's All For Me
(Tune: A Sailor Went To Sea)
A pirate went to sea, sea, sea,
To see what he could see, see, see,
But all that he could see, see, see,
Was the bottom of the deep blue sea, sea, sea.

He dived down through the sea, sea, sea,
And found a rusty key, key, key,
He shouted out with glee, glee, glee
'The treasure's all for me, me, me!'

Puppets

Stories

 Pinnochio Traditional
Act out scenes from the story when the puppet comes
to life.

 I'm A Little Monkey by Tim Weave
Make felt finger puppets of Monkey's animal friends.

 Cheeky Monkey! by Mel Astill
Act out the story of Joe and his puppet Jojo.

Cheeky Monkey!

There were teddies in Joe's toy box, a wooden fire engine, a dance mat and some animal puppets. The teddies were cuddled and taken for picnics, the fire engine was raced to emergencies and the dance mat was danced upon until Joe's feet were sore…but no-one ever played with the puppets.

Joe wasn't careful with his toys. Teddy's leg had fallen off, there were two wheels missing from the fire engine and the dance mat had been stamped upon a bit too hard. "I'm bored!" shouted Joe, "I've got NOTHING to play with!" Joe's mum looked in his toy box, "what about your puppets?" "BORING!" yelled Joe. "That's all there is that isn't broken," said mum sadly.

Joe sat and thought. He peered into the toy box and pulled out a monkey puppet. He made the monkey nod his head, wave his arms, clap his paws and swing around the room. Joe had an idea! He found mum reading a book so he made the puppet pop up above the book.

"Hello", said the puppet. "Hello" said mum. "I'm Jojo the monkey," said the puppet. "Hello Jojo" said mum. "I know a boy called Joe who is sorry for being cross, and not being careful with his toys" said the puppet. "That's good, I am glad" said mum. "Would you like a banana Jojo?" asked mum. "No...but I would!" said Joe leaping up and giving his mum a big hug. "Cheeky monkey!" laughed mum.

Songs and rhymes

● There Are No Strings On Me

Ten Finger Puppets
(Tune: Ten Little Indians)
There was one, there were two,
There were three finger puppets,
There were four, there were five,
There were six finger puppets,
There were seven, there were eight,
There were nine finger puppets,
Ten finger puppets on my hands.

I'm A Little Puppet
(Tune: I'm A Little Teapot)
I'm a little puppet, tall and thin
Here's my body and here's my strings.
When you pull the right one, I'll begin
To move and dance and even sing!

Recycling

Stories

Dinosaurs And All That Rubbish by Michael Foreman
Make collages out of junk.

One World by Michael Foreman
Make a world in a bucket using shells, stones, seaweed and toy fish.

Why Should I Recycle? by Jen Green
Use the information from the book to create posters to promote recycling.

George Saves The World By Lunchtime by Jo Readman
Act out the story of George's efforts to recycle.

Yucketypoo by Jilly Henderson-Long
Design creatures from rubbish.

Songs and rhymes

● My Old Man's A Dustman

Wonderful Earth
(Tune: original)
We all live on a wonderful earth,
Full of plants and animals and people too.
Let's not spoil our wonderful earth,
So here are some things you can try to do.

Pick up your litter, recycle those cans.
Sort out your rubbish and make some plans
To re-use bags and recycle the news,
We can all help if only we choose.

Chorus
Walk to school, and ride your bikes.
Plant some trees and treasure the sights
Of forests and rivers where fish want to swim,
We can all help and we're going to win.

Recycle Rap
See a piece of litter, pick it up, pick it up,
See a piece of litter, pick it up, pick it up.
Cans in the can, bottles in the bank,
Plastic in the bin and paper in the sack.
Recycle, all you can, recycle, that's the plan,
Recycle, all you can, recycle, that's the plan!

Drop It In The Recycling
(Tune: My Old Man's A Dustman)
Turn a tree to paper.
Read it if you can.
Drop it in the recycling
And then you have a plan.
Drink from a plastic bottle.
Save it from the bins.
Drop it in the recycling
Along with glass and tins.
Lots of junk around you?
Look at it once more!
Drop it in the recycling
Don't leave it on the floor.

Senses

Stories

Lucy's Picture by Nicola Moon
Use a variety of textured materials to create a collage like Lucy does.

Who's Making That Smell/Noise? by Philip Hawthorn
Make a lift-the-flap picture of a favourite smell or sound.

The Gingerbread Man Traditional
Create a dance with the repeated phrase 'you can't catch me, I'm the gingerbread man' to chant as an accompaniment.

The Princess And The Pea Traditional
Act out the story. How dramatic can the princess be, as she can't sleep due to a pea under her mattress?

Songs and rhymes

● Heads, Shoulders, Knees And Toes

In My Own Way
(Tune: Oh When The Saints)
What can I see? X2
What can I see in school today?
I'm gonna make a list of sights
That I can see in school today.
Hear, smell, taste, feel, sounds, smells, tastes, touches…

What can I see? X2
What can I see at home today?
I'm gonna make a list of sights
That I can see at home today.

All My Senses
I can spy with my little eye
I can hear with my little ear
I can smell with my little nose
I can touch with my little toes
I can taste with my little tongue
Now all my senses I have sung.
All work well.   X2

Shapes

Stories

Elmer by David McKee
Give children lots of squares and access to lots of different materials to create a collage of Elmer.

The Blue Balloon by Mick Inkpen
Act out the story and use a blue balloon as a prop.

A Triangle for Adaora by Ifeoma Onyefulu
Act out Adaora's search for shapes in Africa.

Shape Train by Mel Astill
Use different shaped sponges to print trains and other shape pictures.

Shape Train

Jack's painting kept going wrong. He was feeling very cross. "Can I help?" asked his dad. "My brush won't paint a train with round wheels, square carriages and a pointy chimney" said Jack angrily.

"But you have to make your brush paint a train" explained dad.

Jack tried hard but it was no good. He felt sad. "Hmmmm…. I know what might help," said Dad mysteriously. He fetched a square sponge, a round sponge, rectangular and triangular sponges and a special piece of fluffy cotton wool.

Dad showed Jack how to print by dipping the sponges carefully in the paint and pushing them on to the paper. "Wow!" said Jack. He dipped the circular sponge in his black paint and printed six round wheels, he dipped the square sponge in his red paint and made two square carriages. Then he dipped the rectangular sponge in his blue paint and made an engine. Dad used the triangular sponge to make a pointy chimney.

Only the cotton wool was left, "Can you guess what that is for?" asked Dad.

"I can, I can," said Jack, happy with his shape train. "It's the steam that comes from the triangular chimney, on the rectangular engine, that pulls the square carriages with the round wheels!"

Songs and rhymes

(including circle games)
● My Hat it Has Three Corners
● Here We Go Round the Mulberry Bush

Stepping Stones to Creativity

- Twinkle Twinkle Little Star
- Ring a Ring a Rosie
- Farmer's in His Den

I'm a Little Bubble
(Tune: I'm a Little Teapot)
I'm a little bubble, small and round
Floating up above the ground.
If you turn me over you will see
I'm still a circle, can't catch me!

A Triangle Has Three Corners
(Tune: My Hat It Has Three corners)
A triangle has three corners
Three sides it has as well
And if you play the triangle
It sounds just like a bell!

There Are Four Sides To A Square
(Tune: She'll Be Coming Round The Mountain)
There are four sides to a square, 1, 2, 3, 4,
There are four sides to a square, 1, 2, 3, 4,
There are four sides to a square,
And they measure all the same.
There are four sides to a square, 1, 2, 3, 4.

Make A Circle
(tune: Oh My Darling)
Make a circle,   X3
In the air.
Make a circle,   X3
Everywhere.

Shopping

Stories

The Shopping Basket by John Burningham
Act out the boy's encounters with different animals
and make up new problems.

The Shopping Expedition by Allan Ahlberg
Use the beautiful artwork to inspire paintings of the
adventures that can ensue when a simple shopping
trip turns into an expedition!

My Granny Went to Market by Stella Blackstone
Add sound effects to the rhyme as granny goes
around the world on a magic carpet shopping for
treasures in all the places she visits.

The Shopping List by Judith Harries
Act out the story.

The Shopping List

Sam loved making lists in his head. He liked to list all of his toys, the names of his friends in Reception, all the people in his family, and even the names of as many cars as he could remember. Sam had an excellent memory.

Dad came in from work, tired and a bit grumpy. "Where is my magazine?" he asked. Sam remembered seeing it in the bathroom and so he told Dad.

Carys, Sam's sister was always losing her things. "Where is my diary?" she moaned. Sam remembered seeing it in the kitchen and so he told her.

Even at school, Sam liked to remind Miss Atkins where she had put things or what they were supposed to be doing each day! Gran used to say that Sam's head was full of lists.

One day, Sam went shopping with Gran. He liked going shopping. He liked the way everything was organised at the supermarket in rows, stacked neatly waiting to be chosen. As they walked up the fruit and veg aisle Gran stopped. "Oh dear, I've forgotten the shopping list again Sam", she said. Sam smiled. "Don't worry Gran", he said. "I bet I can remember everything we need from the list in my head." And he did, even his favourite orange lollipops!

Songs and rhymes

- Hippety Hop to the Corner Shop
- Five Currant Buns in the Baker's Shop
- Simple Simon

Let's Go Shopping in the Market
(Tune: She'll be Coming Round the Mountain)
Let's go shopping in the market for your tea X2
Let's go shopping in the market, shopping in the market,
Shopping in the market for your tea.

We'll buy lots of fruit and veg. at every stall   X2
We'll buy lots of fruit and veg.,
Lots of fruit and veg.
Lots of fruit and veg. at every stall.

At the Supermarket
(Tune: Sing a Song of Sixpence)
At the supermarket
Shopping with my mum
Helping push the trolley
Having lots of fun
Choosing lots of favourite
Things to drink and eat
If I'm good you never know
She may buy me a treat!

Space

Stories

Whatever Next? by Jill Murphy
Act out the story using props such as a cardboard box, a colander, boots, an apple, biscuits, toy owl etc.

Bringing Down the Moon by Jonathan Emmett
Paint different sized moons using fluorescent paint and draw pictures of Mole trying to reach the moon in different ways.

The Way Back Home by Oliver Jeffers
Draw, or paint pictures or design model martians or aliens that the boy meets in space.

Beegu by Alexis Deacon
Create space pictures using white paint flicked onto black paper with a toothbrush. Cut out Beegu from yellow card, felt or fun fur and add him to the background.

Songs and rhymes

- Five little men in a flying saucer
- Aiken drum
- Twinkle twinkle little star

I Went to Visit the Moon
(Tune: I Went to Visit a Farm One Day)
I went to visit the moon one night!
I saw an alien, what a fright!

Choose the third line from these:
It was such a scary sight
Was it green or was it white?
Was it heavy or was it light?
Did it try to start a fight?
Did it scream or shout or bite?

Space is a Place
Space is a place
I'd like to go
Where nobody's been
And nobody's seen
And aliens play hide and seek.
Space is a place
I'd like to go
And look at the earth
The place of my birth
And all the other planets.

Space is a place
I'd like to go
To study the stars
To land on Mars
And disappear in a black hole.

Spring

Stories

The Very Hungry Caterpillar by Eric Carle
Paint symmetrical butterflies using folded paper.

When Will It Be Spring? by Catherine Walters
Create two contrasting collage pictures of Alfie in both Winter and Spring.

Flowers and Showers: A Spring Counting Book by Rebecca Fjelland Davis
Use words and ideas from the book to create a counting rhyme about Spring.

Ten Seeds by Ruth Brown
Act out the story using ten children to be the ten seeds all suffering different fates!

Songs and rhymes

- Two little dicky birds

Spring Cleaning
(Tune: Aram-sam-sam)
A cobweb here, a cobweb there,
A sticky fingerprint, dirt everywhere.
A cobweb here, a cobweb there,
A sticky fingerprint, dirt everywhere.
Spring cleaning, spring cleaning.
A sticky fingerprint, dirt everywhere.
Spring cleaning, spring cleaning.
A sticky fingerprint, dirt everywhere.

Spring Time
(Tune: Flintstones)
Spring time,
In the Spring time,
There are flowers growing everywhere.
Spring time,
In the Spring time,
Breathing in the clean fresh air.
Spring time,

In the Spring time,
Blossoms blooming in all the trees.
Spring time,
In the Spring time,
Listen out for the birds and bees.

Spring Pairs
(Tune: Two little dicky birds)
A chicken and a rabbit
Were sitting on a hill.
One called Charlie,
One called Bill.
Fly away Charlie,
Hop away Bill,
Fly back Charlie,
Hop back Bill.

Two little frogs
Swimming in a pond.
One called Rufus,
One called Ron.
Jump away Rufus,
Jump away Ron.
Jump back Rufus,
Jump back Ron.

Toss the Tasty Pancake
(Tune: Hokey Cokey)
You put some flour in first
And then some eggs.
Add some milk
And mix it all about.
Pour the pancake batter
In the pan like this,
That's what it's all about.

Toss, toss the tasty pancake X3
Knees bend, arms stretch,
Toss it in the air!

Summer

Stories

Sports Day by Nick Butterworth
Write and sing a chant to perform at sports day to
cheer on the children.

Dogger by Shirley Hughes
Produce a drama about losing a favourite toy and
then finding it again.

The Winter King and the Summer Queen by Mary Lister
Create paintings that use colour and texture to
contrast winter with summer.

We're Going On A Picnic by Pat Hutchins
Get children to plan and design their own picnic,
using their favourite food or drink.

Songs and rhymes

● The sun has got his hat on
● We're all going on a summer holiday

The Summer Fair
(Tune: The Animal Fair)
I went to the summer fair,
The sun shone everywhere.
The children played,
The parents stayed,
And everyone was there.
I went to lots of stalls,
Tombola, books and all
And then it rained, we all got wet,
And what became of the summer,
Summer, summer, summer…

It's A Picnic
(Tune: In the Navy)
It's a picnic
The sandwiches are made
It's a picnic
The picnic cloth is laid
It's a picnic
Let's drink some lemonade
It's a picnic
It's a picnic.

It's a picnic.
So come and join us too.
It's a picnic.
With treats for me and you.
It's a picnic.
A perfect summer view
It's a picnic.
It's a picnic.

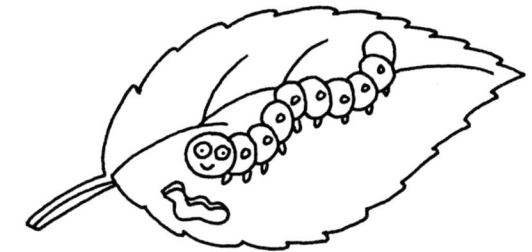

Toys

Stories

I Love You, Blue Kangaroo by E. C. Clark
As the toys build up in the bed sing this song to
the tune of '*There Were Ten In The Bed*':
There were toys in the bed, and little Lily said
'Roll over, roll over'
So they all rolled over and one fell out!

The Velveteen Rabbit by Margery Williams
Improvise a dramatic story about toys coming to life
when the children are not looking.

Old Bear Stories by Jane Hissey
Make a collage out of pictures of the different toys
from the stories.

Dogger by Shirley Hughes
Create a wall-display of a toy stall with a toy designed,
drawn and painted by each child.

Songs and rhymes

- Miss Polly Had A Dolly
- Jack In The Box Jumps Up
- I'm Forever Blowing Bubbles

Favourite Toy

In the toy box, hidden away,
Lies the tatty bear.
Smiling boy, burrows down,
Grabs without a care.
Pulls the treasure to the light
Shakes it in the air.
Laughs and jumps about the room.
His favourite toy is there!

Girls and Boys

(Tune: Girls and boys come out to play)
Girls and boys come out to play
With all their toys they start the day.
Play with a rope and play with a ball,
Play in the sandpit and that's not all.

Girls and boys stay in to play
With all their toys they start the day.
Play with a puzzle and play with a game
Play together and play the same.

The Toy Shop

(Tune: How Much Is That Doggie)
How much is that dolly in the window?
The one with the long yellow hair.
How much is that dolly in the window?
The one next to that teddy bear.

How much is that teddy in the window?
The one with the red spotty bow.
How much is that teddy in the window?
The one next to that blue yoyo.

How much is that yoyo in the window?
The one that that is shiny and new.
How much is that yoyo in the window?
Oh please can I have that too?

Water

Stories

Mr Gumpy's Outing by John Burningham
Act out the story.

The Rainbow Fish by Marcus Pfister
Use lots of colours and one sparkly scale to create
a small collage of fish or one large fish.

The Pig in the Pond by Martin Waddell
Use voices, body sounds and musical instruments to
add sound effects to the story.

Mrs Armitage and the Big Wave by Quentin Blake
Draw designs and plans for a new boat for Mrs Armitage.

Songs and rhymes

- Row Row Row The Boat
- 12345, Once I Caught a Fish Alive
- Five Little Ducks Went Swimming One Day
- A Sailor Went to Sea
- The Big Ship Sails on the Alley Alley Oh
- Jack and Jill Went Up the Hill
- My Bonnie Lies Over the Ocean

This Is The Way I Wash My Hands

(Tune: Here We Go Round The Mulberry Bush)
This is the way I wash my hands
Wash my hands, wash my hands.
This is the way I wash my hands

When I'm using water.
(Substitute face/feet/knees, etc.)

Sailing Boats
(Tune: My Bonnie Lies Over The Ocean)
I want to sail boats on the ocean
I want to sail boats on the sea
I want to sail boats on the river
And catch lots of fishes for tea.

I want to sail boats on the ocean
I want to sail boats on the sea
I want to sail boats on the river
And sail there with you and me.

Animals in the Water
Racoon in the river
Seal in the sea
Pig in the pond
That makes three.
Animals in the water
Lamb in the lake
Parrot in the pool
Make no mistake.
Octopus in the ocean
Whale in the well
Panda in the puddle
Who can tell?
Snake in the sink
Bear in the bath
Bee in the bottle
You're having a laugh!

Weather

Stories

After the Storm by Nick Butterworth
Use wax crayons and bark rubbing to create a giant fallen tree from the park.

On The Same Day in March: A Tour of the World's Weather by Marilyn Singer
Build a mobile to show the world's weather using a balloon and papier mache to make a model globe. Then suspend from the mobile cut-out pictures of rain, snow and sun from different areas of the world.

Snow Storm by Heather Amery and Stephen Cartwright
Act out the story.

Alfie's Weather by Shirley Hughes
Choose a poem for each season and add sound effects using instruments.

Songs and rhymes

- Rain, Rain Go Away
- I Hear Thunder
- The Sun Has Got His Hat On
- Here We Go Round The Mulberry Bush

If It's Sunny And You Like It
(Tune: If You're Happy And You Know It)
If it's sunny and you like it,
Clap your hands.
If it's sunny and you like it,
Clap your hands,
If it's sunny and you like it,
And you really want to show it,
If it's sunny and you like it,
Clap your hands!

What's The Weather Today?
(Tune: Row, Row, Row Your Boat)
Sun, rain, wind or snow,
What's the weather today?
Look out of the window
And see what's on it's way.

Sun is shining high
That's the weather today.
No clouds in the sky.
Let's go out to play.

Rain is pouring down
That's the weather today.
Put on your boots and fasten your coat.
Let's go out to play.

I'll Be Using My Umbrella
(Tune: She'll Be Coming Round The Mountain)
I'll be using my umbrella in the rain
I'll be using my umbrella in the rain
I'll be using my umbrella, using my umbrella,
Using my umbrella in the rain.

I'll be wearing my sunglasses in the sun….

I'll be wearing my hat and gloves in the snow…

Winter

Stories

 One Snowy Night by Nick Butterworth
Act out the arrival of each new animal as they come
to Percy's hut for shelter from the storm.

 The Snowman by Raymond Briggs
Devise a simple dance to go with the music of the
Snowman.

 The Snow Lambs by Debi Gliori
Use different colours and a variety of materials to
create contrasting inside and outside pictures or scenes.

Bear Snores On by Karma Wilson
Act out the story.
 Play 'Wake up Mrs. Bear'. Get children to sit in a
circle with Mrs. Bear asleep in the centre. Give Mrs.
Bear a 'treasure' such as a musical instrument or soft
toy to guard. Can a volunteer creep to the centre and
take the treasure without waking her?

Keep Moving
(Tune: One Finger, One Thumb)
Four fingers, one thumb, keep moving X3
And put on your mittens today.
Five toes, one foot, keep moving X3
And put on your boots today.

Winter Blues
I'm so lonely and cold and it's all bad news X2
I'm gonna sing the winter blues.

Winter Ways
Winter ways
Freezing days
Evergreen trees
Knobbly knees
Starry night
Snowy white
Icy puddles
Warming huddles.

Songs and rhymes

● The North Wind Doth Blow
● Here We Go Round The Mulberry Bush

Trying To Keep Warm
(Tune: Jelly On The Plate)
Shiver in the cold,
Shiver in the cold,
Shiver, shiver, shiver, shiver,
Shiver in the cold.

Trying to keep warm,
Trying to keep warm,
Rubbing hands together,
Trying to keep warm.

Shiver in the cold…

Trying to keep warm….
Stamping feet, stamping feet.
Trying to keep warm.

Bibliography

- *A Bad Case of Stripes* by David Shannon (Scholastic)
- *A Triangle For Adaora* by Ifeoma Onyefulu (Frances Lincoln Childrens Books)
- *After The Storm* by Nick Butterworth (Picture Lions)
- *Alfie's Weather* by Shirley Hughes (Red Fox)
- *Amazing Airplanes* by Tony Mitton (Kingfisher)
- *Amazing Machines* by Tony Mitton (Kingfisher)
- *Anansi The Spider* Traditional Caribbean (Holt & Co.)
- *Another Fine Mess* by Tony Bonning (Gullane Children's Books)
- *Autumn* by Gerda Muller (Floris Books)
- *Autumn Is For Apples* by Michelle Knudsen (Random House)
- *Bear Snores On* by Karma Wilson (Simon & Schuster Children's Books)
- *Beegu* by Alexis Deacon (Red Fox)
- *Big Book Of Families* by Catherine Anholt (Walker Books Ltd.)
- *Biscuit Bear* by Mini Grey (Red Fox)
- *Bringing Down The Moon* by Jonathan Emmett (Walker Books Ltd.)
- *Bumpus Jumpus Dinosaurumpus* by Tony Mitton (Orchard Books)
- *By The Light of The Moon* by Sheridan Cain (Little Tiger Press)
- *Can't You Sleep, Little Bear* by Martin Waddell (Walker Books Ltd.)
- *Captain Flinn and The Pirate Dinosaurs* by Giles Andreae (Puffin Books)
- *Cinderella* Traditional (Ladybird Books Ltd.)
- *Dinosaurs and All That Rubbish* by Michael Foreman (Puffin Books)
- *Dogger* by Shirley Hughes (Red Fox)
- *Dr Xargle's Book of Earthlets* by Jeanne Willis (Andersen Press)
- *Duck In The Truck* by Jez Alborough (Picture Lions)
- *Eddie's Garden* by Sarah Garland (Frances Lincoln Children's Books)
- *Elmer* by David McKee (Andersen Press)
- *Farmer Duck* by Martin Waddell (Walker Books Ltd.)
- *Flowers And Showers: A Spring Counting Book* by Rebecca Fjelland Davis (Capstone Publishers)
- *Funnybones* by Allan Ahlberg (Puffin Books)
- *George Saves The World By Lunchtime* by Jo Readman (Eden Project Childrens Books)
- *Goldilocks and The Three Bears* Traditional (Ladybird Books)
- *Grandad Pot* by Siobhan Dodds (Walker Books Ltd.)
- *Handa's Surprise* by Eileen Browne (Walker Books Ltd.)
- *Hansel and Gretel* Traditional (Walker Books Ltd.)
- *Harry and The Bucketful of Dinosaurs* by Ian Whybrow (Puffin Books)
- *How The Leopard Got His Spots* by Rudyard Kipling (Orchard Books)
- *How To Catch A Star* by Oliver Jeffers (Harper Collins Children's Books)
- *I'm A Little Monkey* by Tim Weave (Buster Books)
- *I Love You, Blue Kangaroo* by E. C. Clark (Andersen Press)
- *I Want A Cat* by Tony Ross (Andersen Press)
- *I Want A Pet* by Lauren Child (Frances Lincoln Children's Books)
- *I Will Not Ever Never Eat A Tomato* by Lauren Child (Orchard Books)
- *I Wish I Were A Dog* by Lydia Monks (Hardie Grant Egmont)
- *Jack And The Beanstalk* Traditional (Ladybird Books)
- *Jasper's Beanstalk* by Nick Butterworth (Hodder Children's Books)
- *Kite Flying* by Grace Lin (Dragonfly Books)
- *Lights Out! Shadow Pop-Up And Play* by Richard Fowler (Barron's Educational Series)
- *Lighting A Lamp* by Jonny Zucker (Frances Lincoln Children's Books)
- *Lisa's Airplane Trip* by Anne Gutman (Alfred A. Knopf)
- *Little Red Riding Hood* Traditional (Oxford University Press)
- *Little Robin Red Vest* by Jan Fearnley (Egmont Books Ltd.)
- *Lost And Found* by Oliver Jeffers (Harper Collins Children's Books)
- *Lucy's Picture* by Nicola Moon (Orchard Books)
- *Mabel's Magical Garden* by Paula Metcalf (Macmillan Children's Books)
- *Mr Bear's Holiday* by Debi Gliori (Orchard Books)
- *Mr Gumpy's Outing* by John Burningham (Red Fox)
- *Mrs Armitage And The Big Wave* by Quentin Blake (Harcourt Children's Books)
- *Mrs Lather's Laundry* by Allan Ahlberg (Puffin Books)
- *My Granny Went To Market* by Stella Blackstone (Barefoot Books)
- *My Mum and Dad Make Me Laugh* by Nick Sharatt (Walker Books Ltd.)
- *Night Monkey, Day Monkey* by Julia Donaldson (Egmont Books Ltd.)
- *Noah's Ark* Traditional (Walker Books Ltd.)
- *Old Bear Stories* by Jane Hissey (Hutchinson)
- *Oliver's Vegetables* by Vivian French (Hodder Children's Books)
- *On The Same Day In March: A Tour of the World's Weather* by Marilyn Singer (Harper Collins)
- *Once There Were Giants* by Martin Waddell (Walker Books Ltd.)
- *One Hundred Hungry Ants* by Elinor Pinczes (Houghton Mifflin)
- *One Snowy Night* by Nick Butterworth (Picture Lions)
- *One World* by Michael Foreman (Andersen Press Ltd.)
- *Opposites* by Nick Butterworth (Hodder Children's Books)
- *Peace At Last* by Jill Murphy (Macmillan Children's Books)
- *Peepo!* by Janet and Allan Ahlberg (Puffin Books)
- *Pigs Might Fly* by Jonathan Emmett (Puffin Books)
- *Pinnochio* Traditional (Paperview Ltd.)
- *Pirate Pete* by Kim Kennedy (Harry N. Abrams)

Bibliography

- *Pumpkin Soup* by Helen Cooper (Corgi Childrens)
- *Rumble In The Jungle* by Giles Andreae (Orchard Books)
- *Rumpelstiltskin* Traditional (Ladybird Books)
- *Sharing Shell* by Julia Donaldson (Macmillan Children's Books)
- *Snow Storm* by Heather Amery and Stephen Cartwright (Usborne Publishing)
- *Snow White And The Seven Dwarfs* Traditional (Random House)
- *Sport's Day* by Nick Butterworth (Hodder Children's Books)
- *Squirrel Nutkin* by Beatrix Potter (Frederick Warne Publishers Ltd.)
- *Stone Soup* Traditional (Child's Play)
- *Tadpole's Promise* by Jeanne Willis (Andersen Press Ltd.)
- *Tell Me What It's Like To Be Big* by Joyce Dunbar (Corgi Childrens)
- *Ten Seeds* by Ruth Brown (Alfred A. Knopf)
- *That Pesky Rat* by Lauren Child (Orchard Books)
- *The Baby Who Wouldn't Go To Bed* by Helen Cooper (Doubleday)
- *The Bad-Tempered Ladybird* by Eric Carle (Puffin Books)
- *The Blue Balloon* by Mick Inkpen (Macmillan Children's Books)
- *The Cat Who Wanted To Go Home* by Jill Tomlinson (Egmont Books Ltd.)
- *The Dance Of The Dinosaurs* by Colin Hawkins (Picture Lions)
- *The Elves and The Shoemaker* Traditional (Ladybird Books)
- *The Enormous Turnip* Traditional (Ladybird Books)
- *The Firebird* Traditional (Tor Books)
- *The Gingerbread Man* Traditional (Ladybird Books)
- *The Global Garden* by Kate Petty (Eden Project Books)
- *The Gruffalo* by Julia Donaldson (Macmillan Children's Books)
- *The Leopard's Drum* by Jessica Souhami (Frances Lincoln Children's Books)
- *The Lighthouse Keeper's Breakfast* by Ronda Armitage (Scholastic)
- *The Lighthouse Keeper's Lunch* by Ronda Armitage (Scholastic)
- *The Little, Little House* by Jessica Souhami (Frances Lincoln Children's Books)
- *The Little Red Ant And The Great Big Crumb* by Shirley Climo (Houghton Mifflin)
- *The Little Red Hen* Traditional (Ladybird Books)
- *The Mixed-Up Chameleon* by Eric Carle (Puffin Books)
- *The Night Pirates* by Peter Harris (Egmont Books Ltd.)
- *The Owl Babies* by Martin Waddell (Walker Books Ltd.)
- *The Pig In The Pond* by Martin Waddell (Walker Books Ltd.)
- *The Princess And The Pea* Traditional (Puffin Books)
- *The Rainbow Fish* by Marcus Pfister (North - South Books)
- *The Shopping Basket* by John Burningham (Candlewick Pr)
- *The Shopping Expedition* by Allan Ahlberg (Walker Books Ltd.)
- *The Snail And The Whale* by Julia Donaldson (Macmillan Children's Books)
- *The Snow Lambs* by Debi Gliori (Scholastic Hippo)
- *The Snowman* by Raymond Briggs (Puffin Books)
- *The Three Little Pigs* Traditional (Ladybird Books)
- *The Three Little Wolves and The Big Bad Pig* by Eugene Trivizas (Egmont Books Ltd.)
- *The Tiger Who Came To Tea* by Judith Kerr (Harper Collins Children's Books)
- *The Tiny Seed* by Eric Carle (Puffin Books)
- *The Train Ride* by June Crebbin (Walker Books Ltd.)
- *The Ugly Duckling* Traditional (Orchard Books)
- *The Velveteen Rabbit* by Margery Williams (Egmont Books Ltd.)
- *The Very Hungry Caterpillar* by Eric Carle (Puffin Books)
- *The Way Back Home* by Oliver Jeffers (Harper Collins Children's Books)
- *The Winter King And The Summer Queen* by Mary Lister (Barefoot Books Ltd.)
- *The Wooden Dragon* by Joan Aiken (Red Fox)
- *This Is The Bear* by Sarah Hayes (Walker Books Ltd.)
- *Three Billy Goat's Gruff* Traditional (Ladybird Books)
- *Tim, Ted And The Pirates* by Ian Whybrow (Harper Collins Children's Books)
- *Tyrannosaurus Drip* by Julia Donaldson (Macmillan Children's Books)
- *We All Go Traveling By* by Sheena Roberts (Barefoot Books Ltd.)
- *We're Going On A Bear Hunt* by Michael Rosen (Walker Books Ltd.)
- *We're Going On A Picnic* by Pat Hutchins (Red Fox)
- *We've All Got Belly Buttons* by David Martin (Candlewick Press)
- *Whatever Next?* by Jill Murphy (Macmillan Children's Books)
- *When An Elephant Comes To School* by Jan Ormerod (Frances Lincoln Children's Books)
- *When Will It Be Spring?* by Catherine Walters (Little Tiger Press)
- *Where's My Teddy?* by Jez Alborough (Walker Books Ltd.)
- *Who Are You, Stripy Horse?* by Jim Helmore (Egmont Books Ltd.)
- *Who's Making That Smell/Noise?* by Philip Hawthorn (Usbourne Books)
- *Why Should I Recycle?* by Jen Green (Barron's Educational Series)
- *Yucketypoo* by Jilly Henderson-Long (Lollypop Publishing Ltd.)